verselets

Akanksha

ISBN 978-93-5438-635-0
© Akanksha 2021
Published in India 2021 by Pencil

A brand of
One Point Six Technologies Pvt. Ltd.
123, Building J2, Shram Seva Premises,
Wadala Truck Terminal, Wadala (E)
Mumbai 400037, Maharashtra, INDIA
E connect@thepencilapp.com
W www.thepencilapp.com

Author biography

A Random young poetry entrant
with vivid dreams to follow, conspiring to become an
author.
A medical student to pursue life in hopes.
Fighting against this bizarre worldly needs.

CONTENTS

Epigraph

These carved lines are to pertain a descent,
lost, spiraling down the soul.

Foreword

If you're someone reading this, its means a lot today.

Preface

It takes days to write a poem, but it takes years to make it
through.
It takes days to find the loose end of a poem yet very often
it remains unended.
Sometimes its magical to read, sometimes a misery to write
more.
All that remians undue is the strength to start it again.
All it takes is to prove this existence.

Introduction

The existential poems,
to the various prospects of life.
The hymns to sing by from the days of melancholy to days of merry.

THE MOCKINGBIRD

the mockingbird

singing the music of life,
wheeling in the air the innocence,
how the world in you, defies.

reciting the melody of caricatured art,
then diving into your own nest,
with thine kindered heart.

the blush of gray plumage,
that causes a rat-tat in everyones heart,
pass through hurry of wind with ramage.

when they say to shatter you is a crime,
they pray for your unimpeachable bliss,
then you sing a song of great sublime.

for you are a symbol of innocence,
the light at the end of tunnel,
of humankind radiance.

FAR BE IT FOR ME

far be it! the fancied world of youth.
when I ruminated thoughts over imagination,
when I pore over words of ocean,
holding an unfolded page of untruth.

far be it! the soft spots of core ties.
when I surmised to have pure blues,
when I to be at a standstill amuse,
sticking for my part as time flies.

far be it! the castles in the sky.
when I scrambled through and through to play a part,
when I crossed a number of spheres to art,
then was the world upside down in outcry.

far be it was me! per se standing on my own.

THE BLUESTOCKING

Time is:
for who are venturous on the air,
feasts eyes on recital,
for who not breathe in oubliette,
with inquisitive mind.
for who trespass wordly goods,
bearing in mind a title,
that said it queen of blues wined.

It is what takes to stand in lieu in believes of culture,
it takes to fly off with winds
when stranded and cast away.
the strength to cease to be out and out,
of every colour,
to all anticipating to leave the nest
you're a blue stocking to portray.

INVISIBLE

invisible
is
that magic flick,
of golden silence,
spaced out on cloud nine,
and escapes into fantasy.
visible
are
moments in the sun trick,
blooming the radiance,
all blue skies line,
and verselets
for our reality.

LOCUTIONS

of that paramour who fosters to be,
arm in arm,
in that world of tranquility.
of that mentor who take heeds to be,
at your wit's end,
brings up advises of reality.
of that misery who comforts to be,
riding on empathy,
that brings the race closely.
locutions of humans
elevates the essence of
Carpe diem.

ANCHOR

How be it comes to you,
When all in all universe defies,
And I wind up my anchor lurching to you.

The anticipation of thoughts deceit my chase,
And this entirety falls nowhere in by-place.

Like a bend and bend over backwards be in vain,
You cradle me, sensibilize this nest-lane.

But this yearning drive to escapade,
Lynches on the wrong side of charades.

And then its your anchor,
The daylight, who pines hopes ecstasy to do.

THE TRIALS

have you touched these blues,
when you sit
underneath this mackerel sky?
or,
watched that brightened star
to be dimmed at horizon.
or
did you wail the grief,
when you feel the
runes of a poem
drawn near your hand?
or,
have you seen solitary,
whilst stagnant in a crowd and
nowhere to hold on?

HIGHER, HIGHER

casted away, higher, and higher,
above the ground, pass the bottom,
in the sky to fly high.

escape the yesterday,
to dive into miscellany of tomorrow.
let the past strings, be singed down,
the existence to hold in hands of our own.

let scars be the beauty of stigma,
so when the season comes, they heal.
to leave the fractured parcels behind,
and to stand in a good stead beyond the time.

step up to this old town,
ride along the shore through sea of changes,
sail to the fate following spaces.

rewrite the book of your own,
follow through drive of spirals,
when the humbled heart be cured,
exit the windows that slammed ago.

to, get away, higher, and higher,
cut the edges, for a new walk of desire.

INTO THE UNKNOWN

Unknown, if there's nowhere to be,,
Unknown, if what this all is untrue to hold on.

but the fragments of this petite heart,
runs a deep down voice, under apart.

it rings the bells, to speak, a thousand words,
only if I could fathom the inner burns.

there's an incite in me, to leave all broken truths behind,
to runaway, endure this reality, find my own kind.

It calls me to stand on my own,
but the past, has scared enough to,
let my thoughts be flown.

It calls me to grow and grow, take a road to unknown,
but the feebleness starts along.
and if all this goes nowhere (into the spirals)
and the end never ceases to rare.

the consequences to all the steps above,
are leading me to higher ground,
what if to fall the roof thereof.

or maybe the sky above is my call,
and the bottoms that echo,
are to be left in these walls.

the only probable my heart knows,
is it longs to go to the unknown.

READ ME A RHYME

read me a rhyme,

when we sit still under the same sky,

when the starry heaven shines the night,

when this rain pours down my window.

for i have been craving this essence,

that adds the heaven to this joy.

The world seems tiny to cease, along

when these blues of nights fade away.

read me a rhyme,

when the slow beat of rain,

brings the warmth sublime.

MY SUNFLOWER

Halo! My sunflower, a metaphor of vitality,
alike this sun you embrace this prodigious universe,
for you gleam this veracity.

here, this golden tinge, brings a word of wisdom,
fosters me to retrieve this passion,
therein this identity of some.

this, the frame of your petals, blossoms sunshine
holding a mirror, to serve a root of
zen to those in the vicinity of us behind.

You, known eminently for protracted stalk,
standing lofty among fellow
in a confident stance to talk.

promising a faith of home.

I REMEMBER

I remember that closed fondness sealed along the core,
yet the openness to be forthright on the shore.

I remember them coddling me always,
being meticulous, so much possessed i was.

I remember those drizzly days,
how far we could go for tiny tea crave in cafes.

I remember chattering-babbling,
across some quotes and poems would win the day.

I remember sledding all over any place,
and no one to wonder, wandering for chase.

I remember those tardy nights, planning to move,
all would remain undecisively concealed approve.

I remember hostility of them, not to turn back,
but those are memory momentos i have.

I remember the earnestness, too close
yet unnamed to other.

CONVERSATIONS IN DARK

as follows these latter nights,
those cines put out on the air,
lying above a dangling chandelier
whew we ran into our own selves here.

belated hours afield from this world, thy to me,
are thou hands lodged with sensibility,
that's when my bosom races louder willingly.

for those gooseberrry bushes
drooping with thy fragrance of sweet,
impelling me to crave this, seek and seek.

let's babble! said thy,
for i deceased with thee utterance,
so much, so many words, still
wee bit this insumerous.

I

I, a pronoun, infinite of probability.

escapes the trail,this melancholiac.

fortuity displays,but I, longs chase.

fatigued off, these pretentious folks.

wept under blue,now eyes barren.

superficially jovial,subtended by dolour.

THE MOONLIT SKY, i

a chin of crimson sphere, i stare upon,

and this moonlit sky beams through the window,

in the silhouette of my own vestige shade.

every night this same old whirling moon, arrives,

yet tonight, a different birth is on rise.

the mere existence of you, is an art

to feel with eyes and to touch with bones.

you, the flowery one, heralds the peak,

of luminescence that heavenly gazes.

the aphorisms of past speak, the day

comes forward with these courts of affection.

this emphatic moon ascends today,

for confessing my allegiance towards you.

THE STARLIT SKY, ii

long I stand beneath this gleaming sky,

the dawn to dusk passes by, to enjoy,

far the misery of a starry night.

oh! these flickering lights, shine next to moon,

from apart the landscape, glows the city,

a thousand lamps and a thousand more dreams.

where to start? where to stand? uncertain aim,

to start journey, where I go the sky stays same.

these constellations shine into the clouds,

and this crescent lunar contour my thoughts.

amongst these nights, there's a falling star that

holds a vanished flame, call it a beauty,

gaze and gaze until nothing left remains,

to watch this eternal realm, lids apart.

WISHFUL-A-DREAM

'A hope' I awaited forevermore,
here, rests me holding void core.

one every time 'a hope' comes,
there it goes afar.

whilst yearning this faith of tenderness,
caught me replaced,
how their inn, flew back, nonetheless.

in expectation, a belief bossom bond
that-one, turtledove, decamped and
went for a sail along.

far be it now,
lie here a wasteland sloped.

hoped and hoped and hoped
what, a co-incidence it occurred?
that ruined it away.

they say, reside again,
who to tell them
there this lies down, in dump to pertain.

it beats me to know
if its gone or yet to come,
or falls apart to lumps.

or therein that petite faith aims
as lets me endure again.

PURSUIT OF HAPPINESS

This pursuit, a question, to live by,
and to fly, with winds high.

when, at times, it is the one being
and their tangible nature,
that unravels the,
hardship favor.

or
it's those littlest things

when,
tiny tea sups, would remind,
halcyon days left behind.

when,
drizzly days arrive,
bugged with profound melody,
that makes you alive.

or
sometimes those strings
you had, then,
olden times that springs.

or that years ago, a desire
to conquer
is contented with choir.

or
this, a very little tale,
that prompts to go
on pirate sails.

and in all these quests,
we live a life,

to find happiness with fest.

OWE-ME-BLUES

when these stars, ripe into
constellations.

when these finer warmth, framed to
Verselets.

when these blossoms, poised in
bouquets.

when these mementos, cast the
silhouettes

when these tiny paces, ring a bell,
of Riverie.

THE FIXER'S

the mentors of vitality

those blossom friendships,
so when pins and needles drive up,
convening a call of trouble trips.

and those sisters and brothers,
who helps verdicts
all those idle times cast at rest.

where secrets and tricks
lie underneath that
timeless carpet,

beneath all these lie
Beautiful ties.

The fixers of a little adventurous life.

OH! ENCHANTMENTS

in the innate dexterity of magic
in an umbrella,
to sing a song of tragic.
oh! wizardry-

painting, an old fellow,
long, flowing beard,
dressed with brimmed hat.~

thick cloak, holding a staff,
narrating Odin the Wanderer,
Norse myths of the deity half.~
for who itself disguised,
to pass, lands of men
unmarked.~

oh! witchery-

an old crone, pointy headgears,
concoct potions in a huge cauldron~
tell-tales! of the witch of endor,
cackling cries,
summoning the death of Mighty Saul.~

oh! Malleus Maleficarum-

inflicting hysteric masses
witches and hunters,
a treatise on witchcraft.~

HOMELAND

down there are days, when selves wrangle,

when our own laughs chuckle,

days of us weeping sanity,

days of errors

here, we share a present,

to be foremost today,

lying here, in these Elysium fields,

besieged by blooming blue-bells,

next to me lie you,

the only blue-bell I put

these thoughts to.

This little heart of you

was as big as the

dawn itself over the wide hills

granting a homeland.

ALMIRAH

a door of sublime opens new realm,

lying in the corner with apparels

untied, glistening the shine over rhymes,

who turned belle to beauty in

this castle of beloved poem of her's.

there lies the thousand secrets of my past,

childhood! the doors to close when I play my

hide and seeks, to open in days of

melancholy, casts my fate to fly by.

oh! the smell of this rosewood remind me time,

when you and I would hide to slide through crimes.

the Merry days of our sheer past recalls our home,

for I would dive again to feel those steps to roam.

this timber glazes shine, tales full of beans.

AN YEAR i

How it passes by,
The time
It plays a merry-go-round
To fly nigh.

A gush of wintery tide
Runs the venules, bites the frosty fingers
And a melancholy looms the month of Jan.

A pleasant parched wind,
the sun shines ten pulses a day
Here, comes compassionate journey
Feb marks, the lovers swirling.

The arrival of spring brings blooms,
blossoms galore and it's sunny and calm with very little
rain.
Comes with adventures await.

The days, scorches the sun
For there is madness in the bushes
Running through petals, a bright side
And a daisy captures the April feels.

There, comes the treasured months

(Junes of July)
The parks, scrambles of pranks
Play these children,
Jesting their glee, for living in a family tree.

AN YEAR ii

Isn't it about the scent of that mist,
Or those dew drops that
Revitalise the futuristic vision,
These rainstorms procure us.

This new adventure of September new's,
We draw an new caravan
Flying with colours.
There's a pinch of summer
Surrounding hues.

An autumn of leaves,
Changing colour,
The trees fall and birds fly,
Us to pertain,
A new October of
Beautiful scenery underneath.

The frosty days come by the bells
They ring for the present to live by
And the happiness to hear by,
From the snow-capes to
Reindeer carts, all bring a merry
For a new hour.

CRYSTALS OF FROST

Ah! here comes a tiny snowflake,
dandling around the wind, shoveling a mist,
rendering the arrival of Christmas and snowy day.

this, a crystal comes with a wintery-tide,
days full of wishes and hopes inside.

how lucky this petite crystal! landing in green
to prepare white,
and we to make mantle of snow throughout night.

the merriment it brings when it dives from heaven,
tell me, if there's anything more than this enchanting
melon?

it hikes around the realm, spreading the spell of bliss,
nay a fence, to swing the dreams of abyss.

Here, it tells a tale, for who builds castles in the air,
are the one's venturing on their own, with grave thoughts
of solitaire.

WHISPERS OF THE WIND

As, when did somebody see you?
as, none.

neither can fathom to see and touch,
only could ambiate this rush within such.

for all overheard the whispers of presence,
blowing birds in vaults of heaven,
tossing leaves to ventilate,
performing the rustles and hymns of forestry
all to levitate.

Ah! like a merry go round you are,
that runs on, in loop-a-loop,
to sail a canvas afar.

Here, you arise with joyous fellow,
murmuring the ferments,
"thee shall rise, for the season is up"

a symbol of resilience, this disclose,
the turbulent vigor of nature evoked,

because the weaklings of heart and soul
are swept by the coarseness of eco.

blessed are those, with unflinching minds and hearts
surviving the bitter crusades of life,
to depart.

the whispers of the past,
telltales stories that forever last.

ASHES; A BROKEN GLASS

a fragmented-glass,

portrays these blues, down-faiths
what a sore sight to remember
the yesteryears proverbs.
the people pieces of these verselets.
these wounds gaping more,
wrecked all sculptures.

an hour-glass,

pictures moments of subtilty.
how this anxiety fills-falls it in,
like the dust dropping out of.
comes a loop, turns upside-down,
here,
it goes, setting starts, top again.

these space-glasses,

prospect's of sheer vastness of
my universe.
how much left to endure!
how much left to unveil!
for lies a deep loop to grow,

a higher ground above,
thorough promises to fill.
believes in future beyond.

THE SCULPTURES

THE SCULPTURES of fine art and verselets,
tinctured with ornaments of unrelenting past of history,
depicting a story of those merchants.

those varied phrasings of inklings ,
written on stones lie through eternity,
cryptically concealed caricatured clippings.

decades of scriptures, handwritings, tales,
sonnets to epigrams to haiku,
muddled with antique history of our present lie
awaits.

PROCLIVITY

Tell me? is there a
dismay of this lunatic poet
and a frantic lover?

this beloved beholds the beauty
of his lover,
stands to walk for
finest-lowest days,
and yet rest besides forever.

this one, sawing-off the half world,
ran into, myriad folks,
yet he searched-to-scorched,
the one he loves by heart.

the nature, seems tedious to him,
but the glints of his beloved eye shines.
crossing all these constraints, vast norms,
of these sororities, redefines beauty,
to dwell in the womb of his beloved.

here, comes a way to this poet.

tell me, does he not scrambles
from earth to heaven, heaven to earth

to seek the phrases to fill his soul?

tell me, is he not demented for his
writings, or,
does not marks endeavor to
preach it to its destiny?

tell me, is it not the same longing
he has for these verselets, when these reach
their winds-up to be?

Answer, if there's a dismay amid
this lunatic lover and frantic poet!

THIS DAY

Here, starts a magnificent Aurora,
To meet us, the fine rain dusts.

For us to ride solitary,
To preach us, for this contentment.

Then starts, our expedition,
To devour this collation.

You know,
What is it that puts together our smiles?
It's the blithe wander, we go through
Everyday.

Be it Those wee-bee blissful rendezvous,
Or these
entangled pinks-pinkies.

This bond has no epithet,
But i to call you a turtle dove,
Amidst blues radiating whites.

This day, has not ceased yet,
There are more winds for us to fly ahead.

HALF WAY

half way through this road, I have taken now

brings severity, to be left behind.

often, I think to be stumbled by here,

if my verdicts, thus sold to reality.

recalling those foremost steps, I walked,

I knew these sentiments leaded my path.

the timber forest along the road, speaks

a connexion I carve with this ride,

the enchantments of this path, bounds me,

rings a spell, as my past wonders back here.

these strings pull me into an unknown bond,

yet so scared to take a step beyond.

half way through this road, I have taken now

Counts, axioms of fortune to come.

FIDDLE HEART

this, fate rings the tales,

of a young heart that prevails.

a puerile soul, oblivious

to the next phase,

yet valiant face to wear.

here, you have an aspiration,

long drawn, to be ourselves

in this scenic station.

keeping this soft core alive,

to dwell home you have.

these dreams, eminent to remain,

neither petite nor heavy,

to do it again.

all you need is a heart,

to conclude, your own,

achieve this part.

to serve this fool's paradise.

SPIRALS OF MIND

if talked about, the minds,
alike this cosmos, adept of vastness lies.

this light, a source of vivacity
lies somewhere, all of us in eternity,
to surpass, these untrue portions
of incidents.

there lies the vacuum of knowledge,
damps the mind with entropies hedge
under all stamped.

the magnetism, to captivate the unlike poles,
to come together of the two souls.

the gravitation force, tempting the moon,
to encircle this earth.
thereof lies a same force,
inside this mind and body pours.
drives this sense, harmonizes the connexion
of parts.

this space, emptied of entire celestials,
alike these brains, promise

these thoughtful potentials.
breeds the house of discovery.

BELIEF

belief, the firm faith, for this sacred holy

reckoning the superstitious feel.

the creed of confidence,

to untangle constraints of ability.

Through the freedom of remarks.

to be in spirit of absolute,

he, who holds reasons for you to be here.

to the questions of you and me.

to be in eminence of someone,

for the one to hold on,

to be together for eternity.

THE DRIZZLED DROPS

oh! to play with this hail!

the amusement it brings to ship this sail.

the sight before drizzle,

brings the furious winds to bristle.

the sky curves dark,

to enchant the arrival of this horizon arc.

this hurricane of sand and dust,

breaches the pine leaves thriving to swirl.

the flocks of fangs fly high above,

the gentle drips descends the heaven up.

the rumbles in the sky mark the thumps

when clouds together strike the bolt once.

In the end, the dewdrops lying in petals,

draws a dazzling sky, thus a rainbow nestles.

INFINITE SPIRIT

there exists an infinite spirit,

for he who exists,

narrates the steps driving off these limits.

to reach in this universe,

sit tight, to believe in yourself, for he does.

when the tables bring mishap, the voids left,

naught to call upon, the home seems theft.

the certain he resists stand still.

the unwritten scripts of tomorrow,

he writes, are benovolented parts of

enthusiastic arrow.

this soul of yours is indented part of his,

wherefore in the time's of solitude,

he still sits.

in the days of obscurity to opacity,

perching on his lap, brings serenity.

string along his steps,

for a novel beginning reflects.

SOLELY

a reminder to those,

trapped in a pound of past,
to those, lost in the world of creed
that doesn't last.

and those petrified to move out,
to trust themselves then
to take a leap of faith about.

at times when to sense solidarity alone,
to times they quit you on,
feeling when those whole nine yards
you stand on your own.

this hymn is for you.

when you're unable to predict yet,
what fortune holds,
these answers lie beyond the process,
stand the set.
believe the tomorrow brings a new day,
new cards, new sense.

accept those days of melancholy,

those of merriment
to those of jumps around trenches only.

then depart out in you,
and to perform these steps,
let this universe lead you
to unexpected road next.

even if its heavy,
just flee further and further.

a part of you,

will fetch the foremost version of whole you,
for everyone rings a string of tales,
and everyone goes through an
unpleasant chance.

but the road you have taken,
will bring wondrous beats,
whatever of you to be awaken.

AXIOMS OF LIFE

there's one rule to live by:
to discover the buoyance
of small matters that thrives.

pray tranquility,to these for ,
all the feed, the hymns,
all the sonnets, amities and more.

the cores of false and inquinate,
arise through lust-thirst.
the more to seek, the more to need infinite,
and that's where felony starts.

these myths are not about heroics,
rectifying the wrongs,
or those combating false that outgrows it.
but about
the truths they deem for, or
the avenue of true fair to bring before, or
to raise the hand of zeal anymore.

thus, the tales reveal, what matters
is not war, or the edge that earns
but what matters is:

the believe that harvests ferns.
faith that deems to enjoy
petite joys,
or the present that bestows
than to perturb of the forth-fate.

so, hold hands firm,
as no one knows what tomorrow brings,
but to know who we are in terms.

be ware, what thoughts you seek,
because they render you what you make,
and what fate of wings you take!

EN ROUTE

every ODE hymns a story,
a tale of someone,
afraid yet valiant to face the realms,
scared of some mementos,
but not their own choices.

inclined to do things,
for what's wanted and escape the false interprets.

and answer these wonders!
too afraid to lose compassion,
yet so poised to the deep ends.

the answers of abandoned questions lie nowhere,
but the lane to this fate speaks we are what we forge the
choices,
receivers of mistakes.

we might not know the power of who we are?
or the forthcoming wants ahead!
but that's the zen of life,
to unwrap and dig up ourselves.

to seek the one aide-mate,
helps move throughout the way.

the disparate paths take away to these known endings.

all to do is reach these fine roads,
and mould these into treasures of destiny,
riding in the full swing.

PAPER PLANES

Life is not a thing like we drew.

Who do we condemn this for,
Ourselves?
For we have moved to become
Someone.

But then here, I'm living a fate
without you,
Because so far, we're not once used to be,
ou,today, are not.

We meet through eyes, at each other, you know,
Like we carved the words already.

My mind wanders off sometime,
If, Is this it?
Where did we reach?
All our dreams and desires to be.

Who are our selves today?
Are we draining? or
These paper planes we made
Are drenching in this swamp,

Leaving all this behind.
Life is nothing like we pictured.

TO BE OWN

Here, I stand per se just,
on the verge of a cliff that dusts.

for, ahead lies a deep steep,
then if to stumble, whom to
embrace this weep.

above, are the fleeting falcons,
oscillating in their own world with wings of albums.

oblivious of the sentiments, that surround them,
rejoicing the pleasures of free rein that stems.

oh! how I fancy more of them.

below, lies this stream,
flowing and blooming the pasture land scene.

yet so coherently steady,
oblivious of the path, some place, where it reaches many.

oh! how I wish if it were me.

behind, here a trail track,
that travels the entire routes back.

voyaging the intersects of borders,
for no one to wonder, where it sails, gathering boarders.

what an entire scenery,
to be an object I wish.

but somehow fate brings me to this cliff,
away from home, nowhere else, to be here, stiff.

with a wonder to cease
what do I do now, for what that ache leaves?

KAFKAESQUE

the narrative holds, an existence, for,

a story of one's own destiny lined.

but here lies the new man of western world,

the slave of beurocracy, he became,

to stand in lieu and move the certain way.

from absence of choices ahead, to live,

to some meaningless virtues of life,

often, we are nothing but mere a statue.

For, who knows what forthcome follows return,

who knows, if this road, you chose lie nowhere,

who knows, if we are oblivious own.

there's no light to shed on to journey length,

no answers to how often ordeals last,

thus snap the tedium's, to delight rest.

ROSES

rose, a symbol of fond desire to meet,

but the thorns render the beloved bleed.

for he who dares not to perceive these,

should never chase the covet of petals.

this petite shrub grows in the season spring,

apprehends the beauty to hold strings.

for these when hung onto ceiling, speaks myths,

brings entirety to sworn the secrecy.

the white petals to bring the harmony,

cleanses the mind, incarnates purity.

it rewinds the spells on this paramour,

wretched in this frantic adore, how be it,

to flavor this essence of love, quests it?

for the world knows, its the language "love".

AVENUE

riding through the routes,

I discovered a boulevard path,

there, departs the intersecting pursuits.

these four lanes, hold the several truths,

for each writes different rumors,

and to step ahead in one, to choose own youth.

thousands of hurdles pass across streets,

yet the alluring seascapes

count the same memories complete.

travelling across the arch

on the edges lie landscapes of memories,

some left behind,

some to move on,

some to rewind.

so, drive quick on the draw,

to the existent avenues ahead,

for its a bumpy ride with twists of fate

Notes

believe in the dreams,
you want to live in.
The opportunities lie near you,
all you need is a hope to live by.